essential careers™

CAREERS IN
CONSTRUCTION

HEATHER MOORE NIVER

ROSEN
PUBLISHING

NEW YORK

In loving memory of Trevor James Moore, a lively and multifaceted construction worker if there ever was one. Gracious thanks to Wendell Cook and Larry Cavagnaro for their time and thoughtful responses. Thanks ever and always to Ron Moore for his unwavering love, insights, and support.

Published in 2014 by The Rosen Publishing Group, Inc.
29 East 21st Street, New York, NY 10010

First Edition

Library of Congress Cataloging-in-Publication Data

Niver, Heather Moore.
Careers in construction/Heather Moore Niver.—First edition.
     pages cm.—(Essential careers)
Includes bibliographical references and index.
ISBN 978-1-4488-9476-5 (library binding)
1. Construction industry—Vocational guidance—Juvenile literature.
2. Constrution workers—Juvenile literature. I. Title.
TH159.N58 2014
624.023—dc23
                                                                              2012043299

Manufactured in the United States of America

CPSIA Compliance Information: Batch #S13YA: For further information, contact Rosen Publishing, New York, New York, wwat 1-800-237-9932.

contents

INTRO

Whether the economy is thriving or struggling, the construction industry offers careers for workers with different skills and interests.

DUCTION

At one time or another, almost every generation has to deal with a tough economy. Jobs may be hard or practically impossible to find, but everyone still needs to make a living, pay bills, and keep a roof over their heads. At first glance, some career choices might seem like they'll make a lot of money, but will they endure?

Every field suffers when the economy fails, but some jobs have more staying power. For example, when people don't have much money, fewer of them are likely to start building new homes. But they're more likely to fix up their homes or factories or make other improvements, such as a small addition. Professionals are always called in for repairs, too. What if a furnace stops working on a freezing, snowy night? A heating and cooling specialist has to be called in to repair it so that the occupants stay warm and the pipes don't freeze and burst.

Careers in construction are certainly not immune when the economy struggles. However, the variety of opportunities in the career makes it a better bet than other industries. Society depends on construction workers to keep roads, tunnels, and bridges in good shape, which means year-round repair as well as improvements. Construction workers are responsible for building, fixing, and maintaining parks and other public areas, too. Some type of construction work goes on all year round everywhere in the world.

Still, it's important to choose a career that you genuinely like. Even if it's "just a job" to make sure the bills are paid, it's something you're going to do all day, every day. Try to choose a career that involves your interests.

Jobs in the construction industry can be widely different, so there are plenty of options for all types of people. If you like to work with your hands to create things, jobs in carpentry, stonework, or masonry might be a good choice. Some carpentry jobs can be learned right after high school on site, too, which is great if the idea of sitting in the classroom any more sounds boring.

Those who like to work on computers and don't mind attending college might enjoy careers such as architecture. If driving large machinery seems like a good way to spend the workdays, consider a career as a crane operator or an operating engineer. Large machinery operators also maintain and repair their machines, so this can be a good option for anyone who likes tinkering on machines. Marble and tile setting work can offer room for a lot of creative design.

Whether you want to build structures that people need and appreciate, enjoy drawing and creating, or like the idea of moving massive amounts of soil and rock with a large machine, construction has plenty of options. The following sections offer an overview of just some of the job possibilities in construction. Read on to discover construction careers to consider.

chapter 1

THE MANY SIDES OF CONSTRUCTION

The construction industry is large, many-sided, and vital to growth and renewal, so calling this career field "construction" is not quite accurate. It's also a dependable industry to pursue a career anywhere in the world. Growing populations require new, well-made homes, not to mention roads, bridges, parks, and public resources. Old structures need to be cared for or even demolished to prepare for newer, safer structures. These needs ensure that construction will remain a worthwhile industry in which to pursue a career.

WHAT IS CONSTRUCTION?

Construction includes any work done to build, or construct, a structure. Structures aren't limited to buildings, such as homes, apartment buildings, schools, churches, stores, and offices. They also include bridges, roads, highways, tunnels, railways, airfields, docks, water and sewage systems, parks, and many other things necessary for a functioning society. The construction industry also entails the deconstruction— or breakdown—of previously made structures. Special workers are needed for this side of construction, too. Other buildings, especially older or historical buildings, also need to be restored, or repaired to their original condition.

A construction worker includes anyone involved with work on a structure. Contractors are in charge of the entire job, from overseeing the work by independent businesses, to making sure it's finished on time and within budget. Sometimes they hire

Any type of work on a structure is construction. Planners, architects, contractors, managers, skilled workers, and laborers are all different types of construction workers.

subcontractors to take care of some parts of the job. Planners, drafters, architects, and engineers are all construction workers. They are carpenters, plumbers, welders, roofers, or anyone who helps a structure take shape. They create iron structures that form a building's frame or beautiful and practical tile designs in kitchens or bathrooms.

Laborers and skilled workers do a lot of the hands-on work at the site. Leaders and managers make sure the construction process runs smoothly. In almost every level of construction, one can work for the government or a small business, or be self-employed.

LABORERS

Laborers are the backbone of the construction industry. Most are "unskilled" workers, meaning they don't have expertise in a specific area, although many have general construction knowledge and skills that help them in their job. Many high school graduates can get a job as a laborer based on their personal experiences. A laborer position is a great way for young, unskilled workers to get started in the construction industry. Most construction work requires employees to be at least eighteen years old, although some states such as New York allow workers at age sixteen with a parent or guardian's approval.

Laborers often spend long hours outside in every kind of weather walking, climbing, crawling, and hauling. Sometimes laborers must stand for extended periods of time. These jobs can be dangerous and physically demanding.

Laborers must listen and follow directions precisely. They work with hand and power tools and help transport supplies and machinery from storage to a job site. Laborers set up scaffolding, dig ditches, clear rubble, and remove hazardous materials. Many serve as aides to skilled workers such as carpenters and stonemasons, providing them with valuable on-the-job experience. Some laborers specialize in a specific kind of construction, while others handle more general jobs.

Labor work may not appeal to many people. The pay for this often dirty and exhausting work is the lowest for careers in the construction industry, especially for entry-level workers. However, laborer positions are often available year-round, especially in prosperous locations. Furthermore, laborers can earn a specific certification, such as welding. This gives young workers a chance to move up to more rewarding positions.

SKILLED WORKERS

Any construction job requires countless skilled workers. Carpenters handle many kinds of jobs, including framing walls, roofing, creating molds for pouring concrete, and cabinetmaking. Stonemasons use their skills to make stone walls, steps, and floors. Electricians, plumbers, heating and cooling experts, and roofers help make homes and buildings livable. Operating engineers use heavy machinery to transport supplies, prepare land for construction, assemble cranes, and dispose of rubble and hazardous materials. Other skilled construction workers include welders, boilermakers, painters, and pile drivers.

Many skilled construction workers have some level of education beyond high school. In some cases, workers complete apprenticeship or internship programs before finding entry-level positions. Some attend a vocational school or college. Skilled workers may also be expected to pursue certification. However, some establish careers based on abilities developed in their personal lives.

PLANNERS AND LEADERS

Long before the physical work of a construction project begins, numerous workers help plan out what the structure will look like. Architects design new structures that are

Architects design and draw plans, or blueprints, for construction projects. These professionals make sure the layout of the structure is both functional and stylish.

attractive, practical, and safe. Drafters prepare drawings and plans for construction workers to follow when building a structure. Civil engineers design and manage the construction processes necessary for the construction of buildings,

THE NEED FOR CONSTRUCTION WORKERS

Where would the United States, one of the fastest-growing countries in history, be without construction workers? Society depends on these and the many other construction industry workers to build, repair, and maintain safe, sturdy structures, whether they're houses, factories, dams, or highways.

On April 30, 2012, President Barack Obama reminded the attendees of the Building and Construction Trades Department Conference, "You represent the latest in a long, proud line of men and women who built this country from the bottom up. That's who you are. It was workers like you who led us westward. It was workers like you who pushed us skyward . . . And when that was done, you kept on building—highways that we drive on, and the houses we live in, and the schools where our children learn."

The construction industry also provides a lot of jobs. In fact, throughout the world, construction makes up more jobs than any other industry. The Bureau of Labor Statistics (BLS) reported the following employment numbers for the construction industry as a whole: 476,300 carpenters, 611,330 construction laborers, 156,260 construction managers, 377,460 electricians, and 199,180 operating engineers and other construction equipment operators. This represents just a few types of construction jobs. Wages vary depending on location, job type, and responsibilities, but the BLS Web site keeps up-to-date averages for wages and occupation growth (www.bls.gov).

roads, bridges, and more. Other construction planners include surveyors and cost estimators.

These workers also supervise the actual construction process, as do onsite supervisors, foremen, project engineers, inspectors, and general contractors. Most of these careers require considerable experience, and some require at least a two-year college degree. Architects usually pursue a five-year degree program and internships or certification programs. Some general contractors start businesses based on years of experience.

EXPERIENCE AND EDUCATION

Personal experience can help prepare you for a construction career. Use your strengths and interests to help direct your career path. Consider construction if you enjoy working with tools, building things, or watching home building and renovation programs on television. Additional clues might be your hobbies and activities outside school and your general likes (shop class, building things with wood, working outside, staying fit, etc.).

There are many options for anyone who wants to work in construction. A high school education or GED (general equivalency diploma) is the best stepping-stone a young person could ask for. Math classes teach how to make quick, confident measurements of materials and other calculations. Technology, woodworking, metalworking, and drawing classes are great preparation for working with tools, many materials, and blueprints. Ultimately, if these classes are interesting, construction work may be a good career path.

Some people want to learn more about the specifics of a job and learn additional skills so that they can start higher up. Vocational schools, also called trade or career schools, offer two-year degrees that focus on the construction industry and

There are many educational options for students who want to go into construction. However, basic subjects such as math are necessary for nearly all trades within the industry.

provide hands-on work along with coursework. At community colleges, students can study for a career in management, such as construction managers. Classes might include technical drawings and blueprints, building codes, and management. Graduates often leave with an associate's degree.

Colleges and universities often require four years to achieve a degree. Although most college degrees focus on a specific subject, or major, core classes often cover a wider variety of subjects. Graduates leave with a broader education than those who opt for an associate's degree. Architects and engineers require bachelor's degrees.

Unions and contractor's associations sometimes sponsor apprenticeships in which students spend some time in the classroom but also gain paid, on-the-job training while working with an experienced journeyman. Internships offer hands-on, supervised training but may not be paid or earn credits toward a degree. Military branches offer programs that educate soldiers during their enlistment, as well as help soldiers pay for their education afterward.

chapter 2

WORKING WITH STONE

Stone can form the foundation of a building or add to an interesting patio or wall outside. Careers working with this basic supply are often readily available. Yet, like any construction job, a slow economy or bad weather can make jobs harder to find. Stonework offers options from practical work like installing cement to more creative jobs such as designing tile.

Most stoneworkers need a high school diploma or its equivalent. High school classes in science, shop, math, blueprint reading, and mechanical drawing provide a great background. Stoneworkers must be in good shape because they do a lot of kneeling, bending, and stretching.

BRICKLAYERS AND STONEMASONS

Bricklayers and stonemasons cut, seal, and position masonry materials. They also prepare and apply mortar. Brickmasons and blockmasons—or bricklayers—handle the same type of work. Brickmasons specialize in brickwork, and blockmasons work with cement blocks. Stonemasons build structures out of stone. Bricklayers and stonemasons are often simply called masons.

Bricklayers use bricks and cinderblocks to create and repair numerous types of structures such as walkways

Working with brick and stone requires workers to be in excellent physical shape to prepare for lots of bending, kneeling, stretching, and heavy lifting.

and patios. They fit bricks together to create unique masonry pieces that fill all kinds of spaces. They also build walls between properties. Bricklayers sometimes create ornamental façades for houses, office buildings, and high rises. Indoors, they create floors, walls, and fireplaces and chimneys. Blockmasons sometimes build walls for large structures, such as warehouses, hotels, and basements. Stonemasons work with natural and artificial stones. They build stone walls outdoors, but they also create interior walls and floors.

Masons must be good at math and be able to read blueprints to bring a plan to life. General laborers may learn bricklaying and stonemason skills while helping trained professionals on the job. Some find apprenticeships through trade associations and masonry unions. Taking mason courses at a technical or vocational school will increase the chances of finding a job and getting a higher starting salary.

PLASTERERS AND STUCCO MASONS

Plasterers and stucco masons apply plaster and stucco to walls, ceilings, or dividers. Plaster is usually applied to walls and ceilings to make them fireproof and soundproof, but it's also used as decoration. A wide flat board with a handle called a hawk holds the plaster, and plaster is applied with a trowel across surfaces such as concrete block, wood, masonry, or wire mesh called lath.

Stucco consists of cement, white sand, and lime. Stucco masons usually use a spray gun to apply it to the outside of a building over lath, concrete, or masonry. They also apply insulation to a building's exterior. Stucco can have a decorative rough look if it contains pieces of marble or gravel. Molding plasterers make ornamental plaster shapes such as a doorway

Some plasterers use molds or trowels in a special way to create attractive or patterned plaster designs. This type of plasterwork requires creativity and care.

frame that looks like wood but is actually plaster molded to look like it.

Some plasterwork can be learned through long-term training on the job, but most learn through an apprenticeship program. The International Union of Bricklayers and Allied Craftworkers' International Masonry Institute includes a special certification in plaster.

THE BASIC BRICK

Masons build and work with brick and stone. They have been responsible for some of the most awesome architectural structures in the world. From the Egyptian pyramids to the Great Wall of China, masonry has created beautiful, long-lasting buildings and structures. Brick withstands fire, bad weather, and earthquakes, so it's no wonder that so many structures last for centuries.

Masonry can be as simple as creating a stone or brick wall to building complicated and ornate exteriors. The basic clay brick was first baked in the sun six thousand years ago. Soon chopped straw and grass were added to help prevent breaks and bends. Around 4000 BCE, bricks were molded so that they would all be the same shape.

These days, brick is made up of clay and shale, and is fired, or baked in an oven called a kiln, at about 2,000 degrees Fahrenheit (1,093 degrees Celsius). The standard brick is 2.5 × 3.75 × 8 inches (6.35 × 9.53 × 20.3 centimeters) long. Most clay is found at the bottom of large lakes or clay pits. Sometimes old bricks from a demolished building can be reused. In Indonesia, masons are experimenting with making bricks out of baked cow dung, or cow manure. These bricks are very strong and take far less energy to make than clay bricks.

TILE AND MARBLE SETTERS

Ancient buildings such as temples were built with marble, granite, and tile. The Taj Mahal was built out of marble as an Indian mausoleum in the seventeenth century and remains one of the wonders of the world. Today, tile and marble setters put hard tile, marble, and wooden tiles on all kinds of surfaces, including walls, floors, countertops, patios, and roof decks. They measure and cut the tiles or marble they need, then arrange them by following a design plan and instructions from architects, builders, or homeowners. A mortar or other adhesive is prepared and applied. The tile and marble are installed in the area and grout, or mortar, fills spaces between the pieces with a rubber trowel. Decorative work such as tile or marble is expected to be in higher demand in the future, especially in expensive homes. Because some of this work takes place outdoors, consistent work is more common in warmer climates.

After graduating high school, consider an apprenticeship through a building contractor or a union. The International Masonry Institute's National Training Center, located in Bowie, Maryland, offers a National Terrazzo Training Program for apprentices.

Cement masons, or cement finishers, use concrete, one of the world's toughest materials, to form the bases for buildings, patios, floors, dams, and roads. Factories, office buildings, hotels, shopping malls, and schools always require good cement masons. Concrete masons place and finish the concrete.

chapter 3

WORKING WITH METAL

M etal can be useful, as the framework of a building, and creative, adding decoration and interest. As with any construction job, a slow economy or bad weather can make jobs in metalworking harder to find for a while.

WELDERS

When heat, pressure, or both are applied to the edges of two or more pieces of metal, they are permanently fused, or joined. Welding creates and repairs products, from household appliances and pipes to vehicles and missiles. Construction workers who do it are called welders, solderers, and brazers. There are more than eighty different kinds of welding processes. Brazers connect copper pipes and other thinner metals with a filler metal that needs a higher temperature than used in welding. Brazing sometimes creates a protective coating against wear and tear. Welding is dangerous work. Welders should wear protective clothing in case of burns and falling objects. They must always know and follow safety rules.

Some high schools offer courses in welding. Otherwise, students should consider blueprint reading, math, physics, chemistry, and mechanical drawing. Entry-level welders can learn on the job over a couple of weeks or up to three years for

Welders fashion metal together using heat from a welding torch. Welders help create critical materials for construction jobs.

more skilled welding. Apprentice programs are offered through trade unions like the International Association of Machinists and Aerospace Workers. With additional training and experience, welders can become supervisors, sales representatives, or welding inspectors. Welding engineers usually have a bachelor's degree. The American Welding Society offers certification programs that are required for certain positions. Some programs offer computer classes that are necessary to learn how to run machines or even robots.

IRON AND STEEL WORKERS

Often called ironworkers or erectors, structural iron and steel workers build bridges, buildings, and frames for tall buildings and skyscrapers by putting in steel or iron beams. They also gather the cranes and loading cranes known as derricks that help move heavy tools and materials, such as huge lengths of steel and iron and buckets of concrete, around the construction site. Ironworkers follow blueprints or other instructions provided by construction supervisors to connect all the steel columns and beams together. Ironworkers also cut, bend, and weld steel using metal shears, torches, and other welding tools.

Ironworkers should be comfortable working at great heights while only standing on narrow beams. Iron beams are heavy, and workers must be able to guide them into place and tighten bolts. At the same time, workers are on their feet for hours at a time.

Most ironworkers begin as apprentices through unions and contractor associations. Some learn on the job. Certification in welding is considered a bonus by employers, as is serving in the military.

BOILERMAKERS

Boilers heat water or other liquid solutions under high pressure to make electric power. This provides heat and power to buildings, ships, or factories. Boilermakers install, maintain, test, and repair building and construction boilers and other containers that hold liquids and gases as well as huge pipes for dams. Some boilers are constructed of metal plates that are so big and heavy, a large crane has to be used to lift them into place. Boilers may be made out of steel, iron, copper, or stainless steel.

HOUSE BUILDING BASICS

Building a house takes a lot of work, and there are a lot of details to consider, depending on the type of house being built. But whether it's a mansion or a simple log cabin, there are five basic steps to building any home:

1. Foundation. Every house site has to be prepared for the foundation, or the base of the building. This can involve grading and excavation with backhoes or bulldozers. Basic plumbing is installed and inspected at this stage. Finally, the foundation—a basement, crawl space, or concrete slab—is poured for the house, garage, and porch. An inspector often inspects the foundation before the next step.

2. Framing. Once the foundation is ready, carpenters erect the frame for inside and outside walls and stairs. As soon as the framing is complete, sheathing, roof shingles, and exterior doors and windows are put in place.

3. Plumbing, Mechanical, and Electrical. Next the insides of the house are installed: water, waste piping, water heater, HVAC (heating, ventilating, and air-conditioning) system, ductwork, and basic electrical wiring. Everything installed at this point needs to be inspected.

4. Insulation and Drywall. All walls are insulated and then covered with drywall or sheetrock.

5. Exterior and Interior Finish. Finally, electrical, mechanical, HVAC, and plumbing systems are installed and tested. Ceilings, doors, baseboards, windowsills, floor coverings, countertops, cabinets, tiles, appliances, mirrors, lights, faucets, and showerheads are all installed. Walls get painted or wallpapered. Sidewalks and driveways are poured, and landscaping is often done. A final inspection occurs at this stage.

Boilermakers repair and construct the boilers with hand and power tools such as flame cutting torches, power saws, and welding equipment. They follow blueprints to confirm a building's pipe system. Many boilermakers are skilled welders.

Boilermaker work is dangerous, so workers must know every safety rule and wear protective gear. Some work might take the boilermaker far from home for long stretches of time. During high school, consider math, welding, and blueprint reading. Most boilermakers take a four- to five-year apprenticeship program, but it takes less time if they have previous welding and work experience. Unions and contractor associations such as the International Brotherhood of Boilermakers offer training.

PLUMBERS

One day a plumber might install a sink and the next day install hot water and steam boilers. Generally, though, plumbers, pipefitters, and steamfitters work with the pipes that carry water, steam, air, waste, or other liquids or gases into and out of houses, factories, or other buildings.

Plumbers are called in whenever a house is being built and wherever there is water. They work wherever there are pipes and septic systems. Pipes that carry chemicals, gases, and acids are installed and maintained by a pipefitter. Steamfitters install, repair, and maintain pipes that move steam under high pressure. Some plumbers specialize as gasfitters, who install oxygen pipes for hospital patients, and sprinklerfitters, who handle fire sprinkler systems.

Plumbing work can be tough. Materials might be as heavy as a bathtub weighing 350 pounds (about 159 kilograms). Plumbers climb ladders and work in small spaces. Some travel to multiple work sites each day. Because most of the work occurs indoors, plumbers can have employment all year round.

Plumbers must be ready to work in small and cramped spaces, climb ladders, or lift very heavy objects, such as bathtubs.

During high school, students interested in plumbing should consider math, shop, chemistry, and physics. Some plumbers participate in an apprenticeship, apply for a state license, and take a test. Others work in the field with an experienced plumber. Technical school is another option. Plumbers need to read blueprints, learn safety, and know local codes and rules.

These are just some of the jobs available working with metal. For example, sheet metal workers make, put together, install, or repair heating and air-conditioning ducts, rain gutters, skylights, and outdoor signs, to name just a few. Structural metal fabricators and fitters make or fabricate parts of metal products. They also fit and position the pieces and make sure they are lined up with the other pieces.

chapter 4

Large Machine Operators

Operating large machines on a construction site can be pretty exciting, but working with large machines can be dirty, greasy, muddy work. Much of the work is full-time, but occasionally the hours can be irregular, overnight, and far from home. Large machine operators work in every climate and weather, although rain and cold can stop work sometimes. Most large machine operators maintain, repair, and clean their machines.

Workers who know how to operate multiple kinds of machines have the greatest advantage and can use their skills in other industries. Some workers might be eligible for the U.S. Department of Labor's Job Corps training and certification in heavy equipment operations. Courses generally take eight to twelve months. Equipment operators tend to have a higher rate of injury and illness than other occupations, but safety guidelines and operating procedures help reduce accidents. Large machines such as bulldozers and pile drivers can shake and bump the driver up and down. These machines are also quite loud.

PILE DRIVER

Pile drivers operate a machine that forces piles into the ground. Driven piles are long, heavy beams made out of steel, concrete,

COMMERCIAL DRIVER'S LICENSE

Some machinery requires drivers to have a special license, a commercial driver's license (CDL), because particular skills are needed to operate them. Each state has its own rules and regulations. Usually, getting a CDL is a lot like getting a regular driver's license, but there are a few extra tests. According to the Federal Motor Carrier Safety Association, states must issue CDLs based on three classes of commercial motor vehicles (CMVs). Generally, classes A and B are based on the vehicle's weight, including anything it might be towing. Class C is based on the number of passengers it can carry or hazardous materials it could transport.

Some licenses need special endorsements, or additional requirements, such as to carry extra passengers or hazardous materials. Drivers must pass a test for each commercial endorsement.

Endorsement	Vehicle Type	Requirements
T	Double/triple trailers	Knowledge test
P	Passenger vehicles	Knowledge test and a skills test
N	Tank vehicles	Knowledge test
H	Hazardous materials	Knowledge test and the Transportation Security Administration test
X	Tank vehicle/hazardous materials combination	Knowledge test and the Transportation Security Administration test
S	School bus	Knowledge test and a skills test

Check your state's Department of Motor Vehicles Web site for specific information about CDL rules and licenses, commercial driver handbooks, tests, and practice tests.

or timber that support walls, building foundations, bridges, or other large structures. Piles can be used under water, and the operators might work on oil rigs.

A "pile driver" can mean the machine that hammers the piles into the ground or the person operating the machine. The machine may be mounted on skids, barges, or cranes. Generally, operators move hand and foot levers to put pilings into place. They also push pedals and turn valves to start power hammers and to raise and lower the drop hammers that pound the piles into place.

During high school, math courses will be a big help. In some states, pile driver operators may need a special crane operator certification or license. Certain states classify pile

To operate certain large machines such as bulldozers, workers may need to receive a commercial driver's license (CDL) or similar permit.

drivers as cranes, and eighteen states require pile driver operators to have a crane license.

OPERATING ENGINEERS

When it comes time to excavate, transport, and grade dirt and rocks, operating engineers are on the job. They also pour concrete and other hard pavement as well as help erect structures. Operating engineers run power construction equipment such as front-end loaders, bulldozers, and tractors, to name a few. Sometimes they operate industrial trucks and tractors that lift material with forklifts and booms. They may also control power equipment such as air compressors and pumps that are on the construction site.

Safety is always on the mind of operating engineers. For example, before digging they must know where wires or pipes might be buried underground so that they don't accidentally cut or burst them. They must always be aware of their surroundings.

During high school, helpful classes might include automotive mechanics, mechanical drawing, science, and computers. Most jobs in this field require some training, such as vocational school, on-the-job-experience working with large machines, or an associate's degree. Sometimes completing a licensing exam is required. Some apprenticeships are available. With time and experience, construction equipment operators can advance to positions such as supervisor and trainer, or even open their own contracting businesses.

CRANE OPERATORS

Cranes often tower high above a construction site. There are overhead cranes, mobile cranes, and tower cranes. Some cranes are mounted on a truck, some move on their own, and others

Operating engineers have a wide variety of job options, from pouring cement to running power construction equipment, such as front-end loaders.

stay on a site where they are mounted on a tall structure.

The crane has an area for the operator to sit, although some operators run the crane from a remote control center on the site. Many controls are computerized. Crane and tower operators direct the mechanical boom, or tower, and cable to lift and move enormous and heavy machines and materials. They might dig out and lift dirt or even knock down walls with a wrecking ball. Using moving equipment, they move loads and containers to and from trucks. Other workers often help direct the operators by communicating with a radio or hand signals.

During high school, consider classes such as shop, auto mechanics, electronics, and science. Math such as algebra and calculus and mechanical drawing will help, too. Crane operators often start out as construction laborers and learn how to operate equipment. Others learn during an apprenticeship through the Associated General Contractors of

Many cranes have an enclosed area for the operators to sit, where they use computerized controls to direct the boom.

America and the International Union of Operating Engineers. The International Union of Operating Engineers is one place to attain a crane operating license for overhead, mobile, or tower cranes.

This section has covered just a sample of large machine operator jobs. In demolition work, large machines are used to take down buildings that cannot be repaired. Industrial truck and tractor operators drive trucks and tractors around worksites and warehouses. Excavating and loading machine and dragline operators use machines with shovels to move material such as sand and earth. Dredge operators excavate waterways. The road crew works on highways, airport runways and taxiways, and parking lots.

chapter 5

BUILDING HOMES

Building a house begins with careful thought and planning by architects and engineers. Once the structure is designed, carpenters, plumbers, roofers, and many other workers get down to business. The number of construction workers needed to build a home could fill a book on its own. This section offers an overview of just some types of work that go into building a home.

Most housing construction workers work full-time, but this can include evenings and weekends. Self-employed workers sometimes make their own schedules.

CARPENTERS

Carpenters generally build and repair a building's framework and structures, such as stairways and doorframes. Others build braces and scaffolding for buildings. This is called rough carpentry. Some carpenters also install cabinets, siding, floors, and drywall. This is called finish carpentry.

Carpenters work on everything from houses and buildings to bridges and highways. They follow blueprints and plans to cut and measure wood, plastic, and other materials. Carpenters work both inside and outside, depending on the type of construction job. They may work in tight spaces with a lot of lifting, standing, and kneeling.

Carpenters often have the delicate job of putting the finishing wooden touches on construction jobs.

The organization Habitat for Humanity has a youth program that accepts volunteers as young as age five. During high school, classes to consider include carpentry and woodworking, math, science, and mechanical drawing. Many carpenters start out as apprentices, but others learn on the job. Apprentices learn basic carpentry, how to read blueprints, building codes, math, sketching, and safety and first aid.

Two-year technical schools sometimes offer carpentry degrees in cooperation with unions or contractor organizations. Because carpenters learn so much about every angle of the construction business, they could become supervisors or independent contractors.

ELECTRICIANS

As long as there is electricity, electricians will be in demand. Electricians install, maintain, and repair home, business, and factory heating, lighting, refrigeration, air-conditioning, and communications equipment. Electricians follow blueprints to figure out where to install heating, lighting, and cooling systems, as well as outlets, light fixtures, and switches.

Electricians may work inside or outside in almost every structure imaginable. Sometimes they have to bend, lift, and kneel in small spaces. Injury such as shocks and burns are common. Even electrocution is possible.

During high school, classes in science, shop, and math will be helpful. If owning your own business is appealing, consider contracting and management courses. Many electricians start out in technical school. Some start out as helpers to experienced electricians. Organizations such as the Independent Electrical Contractors (IEC) group and the International Brotherhood of Electrical Workers (IBEW) sponsor programs for apprentices. Most states require electricians to have a license. Sometimes electricians are required to take continuing

Electricians must keep up with the newest technologies and changing electrical codes.

INSULATION SPECIALISTS

Every building needs protection from rain or snow and heat or cold. A well-insulated structure requires less energy to heat or cool it. Systems such as boilers, pipes, and refrigerated units need insulation, too. Floor, ceiling, and wall insulators put in insulation in attics and floors and behind walls. Mechanical insulators install insulation around pipes and ductwork in buildings such as factories and businesses.

Insulation specialists measure and cut the insulation to the size and shape needed and apply it by spraying, stapling, taping, cementing, and even attaching with wire bands. Some insulation is covered with a material such as sheet metal to give it extra protection from the weather. When walls are insulated, workers put up wire mesh and the sprayed insulation sticks to it. Then a wall of plaster or panels can be put up over the insulation.

Insulation removal is a big part of the job, too. Unfortunately, this comes with some dangers if the building is older. Asbestos was once widely used for insulation, but the material was later found to cause cancer. Only workers who have been specially trained can remove asbestos from insulation. They are hazardous materials (hazmat) removal workers. New insulation can be installed only after all asbestos has been eliminated.

education courses even after they have a license. These courses help them stay on top of new technologies and other information about the electrical codes.

HEATING AND COOLING TECHNICIANS

It's not enough to simply insulate a building. Most people want to be able to cool it off when the sun beats down and heat it when the cold winds blow. HVAC (heating, ventilation, and air-conditioning) installers and mechanics put in, repair, and perform maintenance on air-conditioning and heaters. Most HVAC specialists work in homes, hospitals, schools, and businesses. Refrigeration (HVACR) workers take care of machines that make ice and keep food cold or frozen in hotels, restaurants, grocery stores, and homes. Although they might be trained to work on many different kinds, some specialize in one specific type of machine, such as furnaces or air conditioners. Others may focus on installation or repair.

Most HVAC and HVACR workers travel to different sites to work. They read blueprints and other design requirements to work on the heating and cooling. Most heating and cooling work is indoors, but some systems might be outdoors. Workers may have to work in small, uncomfortable spaces. If they are hired for repairs, it may be very hot or freezing cold.

During high school, consider algebra, mechanical drawing, physics, and machine shop. Some HVAC specialists learn on the job if they have a high school education. As heating and cooling systems become more complex, however, college graduates or apprentices are more likely to be hired. North American Technician Excellence (NATE) is one source for HVAC and HVACR certification. Many states require HVAC and HVACR workers to pass a test and have a license.

ROOFING

Roofers cover the tops of buildings with materials including tar, shingles, tiles, slate, rubber, wood, and even asphalt. Sometimes they spray materials to bind, insulate, or waterproof the top of a building. They also work on swimming pools, walls, and other building surfaces to protect them from dampness and water. Roofing work involves repair or replacement,

Whether the roofer is doing repair or replacement, he or she might work with materials such as tile, tar, shingles, slate, wood, or even asphalt.

so even when the construction industry is not hopping, roofers have plenty of work.

Most buildings have composition roofing such as built-up roofing, which is made up of layers of hot asphalt or felt covered with tar. Sometimes asphalt shingles or rolls of roofing material are nailed or cemented to the roof. Single-ply roofing seals seams with special cements, hot-air welders, and solvent welding using butane or propane torches. Roofers must take special courses to become certified to use these materials. Rows of tile and slate shingles overlap on top of felt over a wood base. Finally, roofers or sheet metal workers can install metal roofing. Some metal roofs are made up of cookie pan–sized sheets of metal soldered together. Standing seam roofing has seams that stick up where sheets of metal are connected.

Roofers get tired, hot, and dirty. They should have good balance and be confident at heights. Math skills are important, as well as the ability to communicate clearly and follow directions. When the weather is bad, roofers may not be able to work.

During high school, students can gain experience by getting a part-time or summer job as a roofer's helper. Many begin as trainees or apprentices, working with more experienced roofers.

PAINTERS

Once the walls and ceilings are up, it's time to make them look nice and protect that hard work. Paint, stain, enamel, and varnish might seem like they're applied for decoration, but they actually protect the surfaces, especially outdoors, where weather can wear them out. Painters may also work on walls, buildings, bridges, and equipment. They apply substances using brushes, rollers, and spray machines. Sometimes old paint must be

Painters must be detail oriented. The result of their work is often the most visible part of a construction project, so the end product must be flawless.

removed by scraping, or the surface might need to be cleaned. Holes or cracks must be spackled, or filled to make sure the surface is smooth. Painters mix colors and oils to achieve a certain color or texture.

Painters work inside and outdoors. They climb, bend, kneel, and stretch. Painters working on bridges should be comfortable with heights. They may have to work in uncomfortable positions, sometimes suspended from ropes or cables. Some painters put up scaffolds, too. Injury and illness among painters is very common. They may fall, strain muscles, or experience irritation from plaster dust.

Most painters learn their craft on the job, but some learn through an apprenticeship. Anyone interested in industrial painting can earn a certification through the National Association of Corrosion Engineers.

Many painters are employed by a contractor to work on new buildings, remodeling, and restoration. Others work in the maintenance departments of schools, apartment complexes, or hospitals, to name just a few. With experience, a painter can become a supervisor, a job estimator, or a superintendent (who takes care of a building).

GLAZIERS

Glaziers install and repair glass in storefronts, skylights, mirrors, or even tabletops. A glazier chooses the best glass for a project, cuts it, fits it to the space, and puts it in place. He or she might file or smooth edges, too.

Construction companies, glass companies, and glazing contractors all employ glaziers. Factories where glass items such as windows are put together also hire glaziers. Work might be indoors or outdoors at a site. Some glaziers drive the truck to deliver materials and supplies to the job site.

Glaziers stand, bend, and stretch all day long. They lift large, heavy pieces of glass and other awkward objects and move them into place. Some work at great heights. This line of work is one of the more dangerous, with chances of cuts from glass and sharp tools.

During high school, math classes will be the most useful. Most glaziers start out as helpers on the job with local contractors or unions, but they must complete a training program or a three-year apprenticeship.

This is just an overview of some of the major jobs that help build a house. Drywall installers measure and put in sheetrock (layers of plaster sandwiched between two sheets of thick paper) for walls and ceilings. Floor installers put down blocks, strips, or sheets of floor coverings. These coverings usually make the floors easier to stand and walk on (shock absorbing), keep them from making too much noise, and make them look nice. Carpet installers are responsible for plush floor coverings in all kinds of buildings. Larger buildings, such as apartment complexes and factories, need elevators installed.

chapter 6

PLANNERS, LEADERS, AND MANAGERS

Planners, leaders, and managers have more experience on the job and/or years of secondary education. These positions come with more responsibilities, higher stress, and sometimes longer hours, but they're often compensated with higher salaries.

ARCHITECTS

Architects help plan and design buildings where people live, work, relax, and worship. They work together with clients to plan and design buildings. In general, architects focus on buildings and other structures, from a small entryway to an entire college campus. They must consider the safety of everyone who will be in and around the building.

Landscape architects design beautiful yet useful land areas, such as gardens, playgrounds, or highways. They plan locations for buildings, roadways, and walkways, as well as where to plant trees and flowers. Sometimes landscape architects help design areas that need to be restored, such as wetlands. This is called environmental remediation.

Architects mostly work in offices, but they do visit job sites to check on work progress. Many architects work more than fifty hours each week, according to the U.S. Bureau of Labor Statistics.

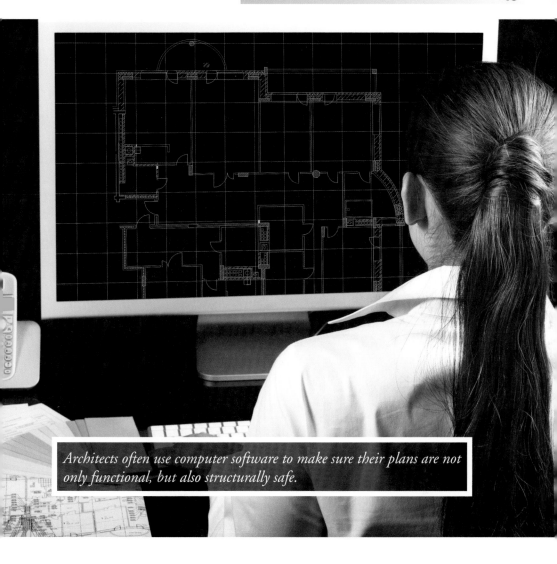

Architects often use computer software to make sure their plans are not only functional, but also structurally safe.

During high school, helpful classes include mechanical drawing, art, history, physics, and math. Some students can find part-time jobs in architectural firms. Many students study to earn a professional degree from a program approved by the National Architectural Accrediting Board (NAAB). All students must take part in the Intern Development Program (IDP), pass the Architect Registration Exam (ARE), and get a license.

EXCELLENT ENGINEERS

Civil engineering includes so many fields that most people decide to specialize in just one. Structural engineers plan and evaluate large-scale projects such as tunnels to make sure they're safe and secure. They usually create the designs by working with architects. Structural engineers often specialize in an engineering field, such as buildings, bridges, or pipelines. They may also work in research or teach. Structural engineers get to spend a lot of time outdoors on worksites. CNN has listed civil engineering and structural engineering as two of the best, fastest-growing jobs in the country.

Civil engineering technicians help civil engineers organize and create construction projects, including bridges, highways, and other significant structures. They also help with land development. A licensed civil engineer supervises the civil engineering technician.

Geotechnical engineers make sure the foundations on which structures will be built are solid. They study how the earth—soil, water, and rocks—will withstand the buildings and bridges built on it by engineers. They also make plans for tunnels and retaining walls, which hold back soil or water. Geotechnical engineers also deal with issues surrounding landslides, soil erosion, and earthquakes.

Transportation engineers create transportation systems such as highways, airways, and railroad systems. They draw and review plans for transportation projects and check calculations. Transportation engineers often oversee these projects.

DRAFTERS

Once the engineer or architect has a design ready, the drafter, or CADD operator, steps in. Drafters use computer-aided design and drafting (CADD) software to make drawings and convert them into technical designs and plans used in construction and production. Their drawings have to show exact measurements, materials, and instructions.

Drafters work at computers most of the time. They usually work full-time, and overtime is fairly common. Most drafters work for engineering and drafting services companies and architectural and landscape businesses.

During high school, consider classes such as mathematics, science, computer technology, design, computer graphics, and drafting. Drafters are more likely to be hired with a postsecondary education in drafting, such as an associate's degree. The American Design Drafting Association (ADDA) offers drafting certification programs. Technical schools, community colleges, and the armed forces are all possible sources for education. (Experts warn that the quality may vary between these programs, so be sure to do some research.) With experience, one might be able to advance to become a supervisor.

CIVIL ENGINEERS

Civil engineers research, plan, design, and supervise large-scale construction jobs such as power plants and roads. Thousand of people may use their creations, so civil engineers must create exact plans. Civil engineers work in the office but check on job progress at the construction site. Researchers may work in a laboratory.

In high school, courses such as math, science, English, social studies, and computers are useful. Internships may be available at engineering firms, local planning offices, and construction companies. The National Association of Colleges and Employers College Placement Council is a good place to start looking.

Civil engineering technicians should earn an associate's degree. Civil engineers generally need a bachelor's degree.

Professional engineers must attend a school accredited by ABET (previously known as the Accreditation Board for Engineering and Technology). They must train in the field and get their civil engineering license.

CONTRACTORS

Contractors—also called construction managers, general contractors, project managers, foremen, or project engineers—oversee a construction project from (just about) beginning to end and keep it on schedule. They often bid on jobs and must figure out what tools, equipment, and materials to use.

Some contractors work on many different kinds of projects, but most specialize in residential, commercial, and industrial structures. On large projects, several foremen may be hired to work on different parts of it. Because contractors work on many stages of a project, they're responsible for hiring workers to do each part, such as electricians, carpenters, and

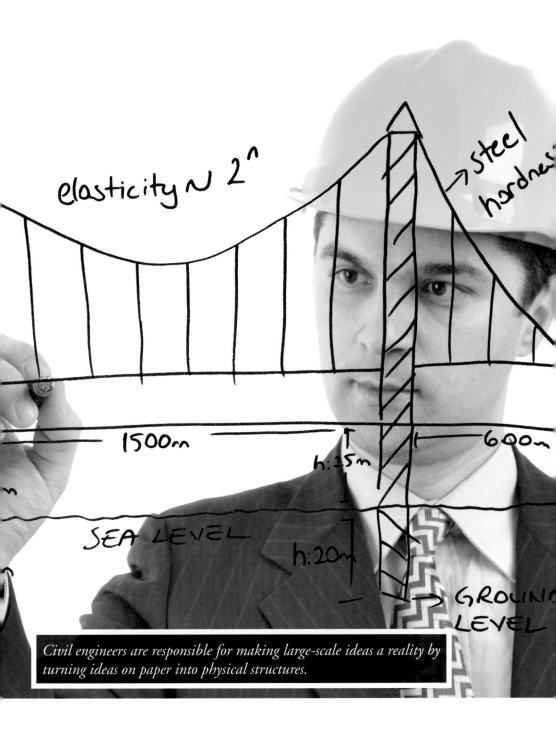

elasticity $\sim 2^\wedge$

$\rightarrow$ steel hardness

—— 1500m ——

h:25m

600m

SEA LEVEL

h:20m

$\rightarrow$ GROUND LEVEL

Civil engineers are responsible for making large-scale ideas a reality by turning ideas on paper into physical structures.

masons. Independent contractor Larry Cavagnaro says, "I meet and work with a lot of interesting people, and I get to work on really great sites with nice houses. Each day is different."

Many contractors use computer software to help plan out costs and time. Often they work out of a temporary office, or field office, on or near a job site, so that they can keep track of progress and be available when problems come up. They might travel a lot if they're working on several projects at once.

High school students should take classes such as art, math, science, woodworking, drafting, and welding. Cavagnaro worked with a builder during summers and on weekends when he was in high school. Some hard workers can become project managers with a high school diploma and years of experience on the job, but employers prefer a bachelor's degree in management, construction science, architecture, or civil engineering. A master's degree paired with years of construction experience may land you a job supervising large-scale projects for big construction companies. The American Institute of Constructors and the Construction Management Association of America both offer certificate options.

COST ESTIMATORS

Every construction job needs an estimate of how much time, money, materials, and labor will be needed. Cost estimators answer those questions to help businesses and managers decide whether or not to build a structure. They also figure out whether or not a job is making money. Most cost estimators work in the construction industry, but some work in manufacturing or other services.

Cost estimators need to make accurate estimates because several other contractors may be bidding for the same job. Usually the company that makes the lowest bid gets the job to do the work. Cost estimators need to consider every aspect of the work. Ron Moore, general manager of Western Building

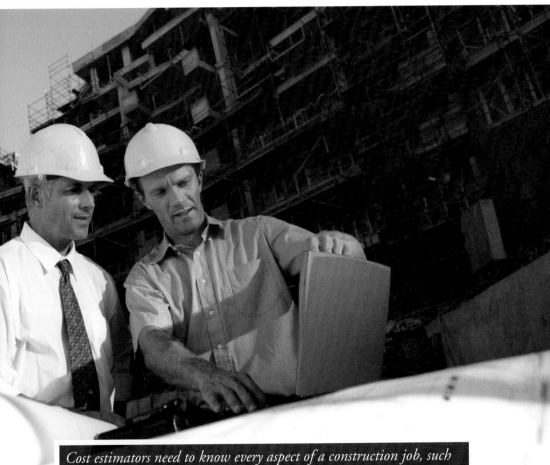

Cost estimators need to know every aspect of a construction job, such as the amount of money, time, materials, and labor it will take to complete the job and make a profit.

Restoration Company, also does cost estimates. An estimator has "to figure the cost of the job high enough to make a profit, but low enough to be awarded the project," he says. If an estimator's bid is too high, the company may not get the job. If it's too low, the company risks losing money when the project is done.

Cost estimators mostly work at the office in front of a computer, but they often travel to the worksite. They work under a lot of stress to meet deadlines with good estimates.

During high school, consider classes in math and accounting, as well as reading plans, blueprints, mechanical drawing, computers, and drafting. Most cost estimators have a college degree in building construction, building science, construction management, architecture, or engineering. If they do not have a college degree, Moore suggests "hands-on experience in the trades of the field."

CONSTRUCTION AND BUILDING INSPECTORS

Construction and building inspectors make sure that all construction work follows local and national regulations. All repairs, changes, and new construction on buildings, bridges, homes, and highways, as well as electrical work, elevators, and plumbing, must be legal

and safe. Wendell Cook, a self-employed home inspector, says, "I inspect homes looking for defects [and] items in need of repair or replacement, and describe needed maintenance." Usually inspections occur at the beginning of construction

Building and construction inspectors check out both old and new buildings in all stages of work. They look for problems, point out what needs repair, and make suggestions for maintenance.

with follow-up inspections as progress is made and a final inspection when the work is completed.

Most of an inspector's time is spent outdoors at job sites, but he or she also spends time in the office reviewing plans and blueprints and scheduling appointments. He or she may have to climb ladders or wriggle through small, cramped spaces.

During high school, classes such as drafting, algebra, geometry, shop, and English are helpful. Inspectors usually need a lot of experience in the construction industry, which can be learned on the job. Some learn building codes and standards on their own or work with experienced inspectors. Cook suggests, "Learn everything you can about 'how a home works,' [and] if possible, find a mentor who will train and teach you."

Many employers prefer an apprenticeship or an associate's or bachelor's degree that includes courses in building inspection, home inspection, construction technology, and drafting. Many states require inspectors to be licensed or certified by associations such as the International Code Council or the International Association of Electrical Inspectors. Cook takes continuing education courses to maintain his license.

Plenty of other upper-level jobs are available in construction. For example, before the first bulldozer hits the soil, the land must be studied. It must be mapped and measured to show precisely what it looks like and what, if anything, should be changed for construction to start. The exact position of a building must be marked. The construction surveyor works with civil engineers, landscape architects, and other planners to map out the property and locate the boundaries.

chapter 7

FINDING AND KEEPING A CONSTRUCTION JOB

In any field of construction, at some point you'll have to search and apply for a job. Once you land that job, it's important to know how to keep it. The résumé and cover letter are important during the job search. A cover letter is a first impression, so it should be professional and well written. Although a résumé outlines education and work experience, a cover letter is an opportunity to expand on that. If you have a mutual acquaintance, or if you know someone who already works there, a cover letter is the perfect time to mention it.

If you have some experience, a résumé is the best way to showcase it. It should be brief and to the point, so one page is usually enough. It's good to start out listing your work experience, beginning with your most recent work. The same goes for listing job responsibilities and specific qualifications or specialties. For samples of different styles of résumés, there are plenty of examples online. The job Web site Monster.com even has sample résumés for all kinds of construction jobs.

For those without education or much experience, all hope is not lost. A broadcast letter can be used in place of a résumé. It provides a brief overview of one's skills and talents. Broadcast letters can also come in handy when changing to a completely new career. A CV (curriculum vitae) is another option. A CV is a short list of basic information

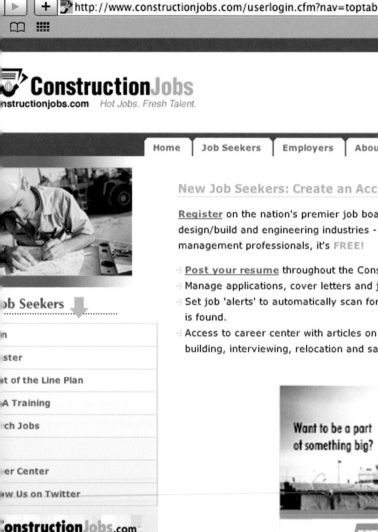

http://www.constructionjobs.com/userlogin.cfm?nav=toptab

ConstructionJobs
nstructionjobs.com *Hot Jobs. Fresh Talent.*

Home | Job Seekers | Employers | About Us | My Account | Career Cente

New Job Seekers: Create an Account

Register on the nation's premier job board and resume database for the con design/build and engineering industries - from trades and entry-level; to mid management professionals, it's FREE!

⟐ Post your resume throughout the Construction Jobs Career Network.

⟐ Manage applications, cover letters and job searches within your free accoun

⟐ Set job 'alerts' to automatically scan for targeted openings and receive an e is found.

⟐ Access to career center with articles on career management, job search str building, interviewing, relocation and salary.

Job Seekers ⬇

n

ster

t of the Line Plan

A Training

ch Jobs

er Center

w Us on Twitter

ConstructionJobs.com
Front of the Line Plan

Want to be a part of something big?

JOIN US.
Click here to search our jobs.

PENHALL
COMPANY
North America's Concrete Professionals since 1957

Signing up for Web sites such as ConstructionJobs (www.constructionjobs.com) allows job seekers to look for work in their field, receive e-mail updates about job openings, and post résumés for employers to review.

about your work, talents, and experience.

Make sure all information on your résumé is true and can be backed up. Most employers do a background check, including online searches. Any false information will give a poor impression and could cost you the job.

Using professional language, proper grammar, and correct spelling shows you're serious about the job. Proofread any letters, notes, or résumés for spelling and grammar before they're sent out. Slowly and carefully read the text out loud. Have someone you trust listen to you read the letter out loud, and have him or her read it, too. Another person might see or hear mistakes.

HOW TO ACT DURING AN INTERVIEW

Once you've gotten a call for an interview, research the company. Study the company's

During the interview process, one should be respectful and listen but also ask questions and show interest in the company and what it does.

history, structure, and what it does. This helps decide how your skills will benefit it. Be sure to work this knowledge into the interview. Of course, make sure your outfit and shoes are clean. Even though most construction work is dirty, you should still dress to impress at the interview. It's important to make a good first impression.

Have a few questions ready to ask during the meeting. Ask questions to get a sense of what it's like to work at the company, as well as what the other employees are like. In addition to helping you understand the company, asking questions shows that you're interested in them, too.

Bring all your important papers to the interview. These can include copies of your résumé and cover letter, high school or college transcripts, or certificates that prove any

KEEPING CLASSY ON THE CONSTRUCTION SITE

Once the job offer comes in, you're on your way. Don't take it for granted, though. Even though a lot of construction work is rough and dirty, that's no excuse to act unprofessional. Workers who show up late or unprepared, don't finish their work on time, and miss meetings are not likely to be given more responsibility or advance in the company. Whether you work on the construction site or choose a career that means more time in the office, Monster.com offers basic guidelines to help any worker get ahead:

- **Do your work well.** Do a good job and be thorough.
- **Be reliable.** Always show up on time and make sure to meet deadlines.
- **Be honest.** "Honesty is the best policy" is a well-known saying for a good reason. Coworkers and supervisors like to know they can trust other employees.
- **Respect others.** Treat everyone at the workplace well because everyone has an important part of the job to do.
- **Stay current.** Always look for ways to learn more, whether it's about new tools, new techniques, or new technologies.
- **Be positive.** In general, try to have a good attitude and look for ways to solve problems when they come up.
- **Be supportive.** When others have helped make a successful job happen, make sure they get credit. Teach others what you know.
- **Focus.** Everyone has a lot going on outside of work, but try to let these things go during work hours. Attend to personal matters on breaks if necessary.
- **Be a good listener.** Let others have their say and explain their thoughts and ideas.

certifications you might have. Before the interview, consider asking former managers or bosses to write letters of recommendation. These could discuss your hard work or other good qualities on the job.

During the interview, use your best manners, speak clearly, and be polite. Consider practicing a few lines to introduce yourself. Some people like to prepare an elevator pitch. Also known as a personal brand statement or a thirty-second commercial, it's just a two- or three-sentence speech to have ready when someone asks you to tell him or her about yourself. It should combine your interests and strengths, some background, and why you are interested in working in the construction industry. This may also help you relax when you start the interview. It helps some people to practice not only their elevator pitch but also their interview skills. Have a friend or family member pretend to interview you so that you can practice introducing yourself, answering questions, and asking questions.

CHOOSING CONSTRUCTION

The construction industry creates structures that are important in our society. Workers have opportunities to build or design; work indoors, outdoors, or both; and help create massive campuses or simple but lovely homes. This line of work offers job opportunities that can be started right after high school or after several years of secondary education. The U.S Bureau of Labor Statistics Web site offers up-to-date salary information, as well as predictions about each occupation's future.

Economies around the world are able to keep humming, thanks in part to construction work. The U.S. Census Bureau reports that 689,000 new homes were built at the time of this writing. In Canada, construction provides 1.26 million,

With countless new homes built each year, the construction industry will continue to provide opportunities for people of all interests and skill levels.

or about 7 percent, of the country's jobs, according to the Canadian Construction Association. With patience and diligence, construction work can become a fulfilling career. Knowing you've helped put a family into their first house, construct a cutting-edge building with the latest technologies, or renovate a structure that might last another century or more can be satisfying reasons for choosing a construction career.

glossary

accredited Given official authorization that standards have been met.

adhesive A sticky substance used to join things together.

blueprint A detailed plan, sometimes a print of a photograph, used to copy maps, technical drawings, or architectural plans.

boom A long arm called a beam that extends upward at an angle to guide or support objects being moved.

certification Proof that one has met special qualifications in a field of study.

drywall A type of board made out of plaster, often used to build the inside walls of houses.

enlistment Time served in the military.

excavate To create a hole by cutting, digging, or scooping, usually using a large machine.

façade The face or front of a building, often facing the road or street.

grading Leveling off or smoothing a surface.

insulation The material used to prevent the transfer of heat, cold, or noise. It is sometimes made up of acrylic, Styrofoam, and chemicals.

journeyman A trained worker.

mausoleum A large tomb, usually a grand stone building.

mortar A combination of cement, sand, and water that keeps stones in place when it dries.

scaffolding A temporary or movable framework or platform usually made of wood planks and metal poles that helps workers reach sites above ground level.

septic Describing systems used to remove waste from a building.

solvent Usually a liquid substance used to dissolve another substance.

steam boiler A container that boils water to create steam.

stucco A mixture of cement, lime, and sand.

subcontractor A person or business that works for a company as part of a larger project.

union An organized group of workers joined to protect their rights; sometimes called a labor union.

ventilate To cause fresh air to move through an area.

vocational Describing education or training aimed at skills for a specific occupation.

for more information

American Council for Construction Education (ACCE)
1717 N. Loop 1604 E, Suite 320
San Antonio, TX 78232
(210) 495-6161
Web site: http://www.acce-hq.org
The American Council for Construction Education promotes
construction education and research programs around the
world. Its site offers links to accreditation programs,
assistance with the accreditation process, and career
resources.

American Design Drafting Association (ADDA)
105 E. Main Street
Newbern, TN 38059
(731) 627-0802
Web site: http://www.adda.org
The American Design Drafting Association, the earliest
known drafting association, offers information on drafting
accreditation, certification, and other continuing education options, as well as employment and news.

American Society of Civil Engineers (ASCE)
1801 Alexander Bell Drive
Reston, VA 20191
(800) 548-2723
Web site: http://www.asce.org
The American Society of Civil Engineers is the oldest engineering society in the United States. It provides access to
continuing education and research tools, the latest news,
and career resources.

Associated General Contractors of America
2300 Wilson Boulevard, Suite 400
Arlington, VA 22201
(703) 548-3118
Web site: http://www.agc.org
The Associated General Contractors of America (AGC) offers
   education opportunities and event listings as well as up-to-
   date articles on the latest topics. A student chapter
   connects students and young professionals with leaders in
   the industry as well as provides connections to schools
   with two- and four-year programs.

Canadian Construction Association (CCA)
1900-275 Slater Street
Ottawa, ON K1P 5H9
Canada
(613) 236-9455
Web site: http://www.cca-acc.com
The Canadian Construction Association strives to represent
   Canada's construction industry. It provides access to docu-
   ments, guides, and regulations; public policy updates; and
   training opportunities.

Canadian Construction Women
142 – 757 West Hastings Street, Suite 290
Vancouver, BC V6C 1A1
Canada
Web site: http://www.constructionwomen.org
Canadian Construction Women is an organization that offers
   support for women in the construction industry through
   resources, events, and the latest construction news.

Home Builders Institute (HBI)
1090 Vermont Avenue NW, Suite 600

Washington, DC 20005
(202) 371-0600
Web site: http://www.hbi.org
The Home Builders Institute is part of the National
  Association of Home Builders. It offers education and
  training, such as apprenticeship programs, for anyone
  interested in construction careers.

U.S. Department of Labor
Office of Apprenticeship Training, Employer and
  Labor Services
Frances Perkins Building
200 Constitution Avenue NW
Washington, DC 20210
(877) US-2JOBS (872-5627)
Web site: http://www.doleta.gov
The U.S. Department of Labor Office of Apprenticeship
  Training, Employer and Labor Services provides informa-
  tion on apprenticeships, grants, and job openings. The
  Web site also has links for youth and teens, as well as for
  those interested in learning about Job Corps.

WEB SITES

Due to the changing nature of Internet links, Rosen
Publishing has developed an online list of Web sites related to
the subject of this book. This site is updated regularly. Please
use this link to access the list:

http://www.rosenlinks.com/ECAR/Const

for further reading

Champney, Jan. *Building.* Brighton, England: Franklin Watts, 2008.

Cohn, Jessica. *Architect.* North Mankato, MN: Cherry Lake Publishing, 2009.

Craats, Rennay. *Science Q&A: Construction.* New York, NY: Weigl Publishers, 2008.

Dreier, David. *Be a Demolition Engineer.* New York, NY: Gareth Stevens Publishing, 2008.

Gregory, Josh. *Plumber.* North Mankato, MN: Cherry Lake Publishing, 2011.

Guillain, Charlotte. *Jobs If You Like...Building Things.* Chicago, IL: Heinemann Library, 2012.

Horn, Geoffrey M. *Construction Worker.* New York, NY: Gareth Stevens Publishing, 2008.

Hull, Robert. *Stonemason.* Mankato, MN: Smart Apple Media, 2008.

Johnson, David, and Scott Gibson. *Green from the Ground Up: Sustainable, Healthy, and Energy-Efficient Home Construction.* Newtown, CT: The Taunton Press, 2008.

Jones, Roger. *Real Life Guides: Electrician.* Richmond, England: Trotman Publishing, 2008.

Kelsey, John. *Woodworking.* East Petersburg, PA: Fox Chapel Publishing, 2008

Kerns, Ann. *Seven Wonders of Architecture.* Minneapolis, MN: Lerner Publishing, 2010.

Latham, Donna. *Bridges and Tunnels: Investigate Feats of Engineering with 25 Projects.* Chicago, IL: Nomad Press, 2012.

Masters, Nancy Robinson. *Heavy Equipment Operator.* North Mankato, MN: Cherry Lake Publishing, 2010.

Overcamp, David. *Electrician*. New York, NY: Rosen Publishing, 2008.

Somervill, Barbara A. *Green General Contractor*. New York: Gareth Stevens Publishing, 2011.

Thompson, Lisa. *Hard Hat Area: Have You Got What It Takes to Be a Contractor?* Minneapolis, MN: CompassPoint Books, 2008.

Weitzman, David. *Skywalkers: Mohawk Ironworkers Build the City*. New York, NY: Flash Point, 2010.

Wolny, Philip. *High-Risk Construction Work: Life Building Skyscrapers, Bridges, and Tunnels*. New York, NY: Rosen Publishing, 2009.

Yudelson, Jerry. *Green Building A to Z: Understanding the Language of Green Building*. Gabriola Island, BC, Canada: New Society Publishers, 2007.

bibliography

Apel, Melanie Ann. *Careers in the Building and Construction Trades*. New York, NY: Rosen Publishing, 2005.

Bureau of Labor Statistics, U.S. Department of Labor. "Construction and Extraction Occupations." Retrieved September 30, 2012 (http://www.bls.gov/ooh /construction-and-extraction/home.htm).

Canadian Construction Association. "Careers in Civil Construction." Retrieved September 30, 2012 (http:// www.careersincivilconstruction.ca).

Career Planner. "Metal Fabricator, Structural Metal Product." Retrieved September 30, 2012 (http://job-descriptions. careerplanner.com/Metal-Fabricators-Structural-Metal-Products.cfm).

Careers in Construction. "Pick a Career." Retrieved September 30, 2012 (http://www.careersinconstruction.ca/careers).

Cavagnaro, Larry R. (owner, Cavagnaro Construction Co., Inc.). Interview with the author, September 30, 2012.

Cook, Wendell F. (owner, Wendell F. Cook Home Inspections). Interview with the author, September 24, 2012.

Eberts, Marhorie, and Margaret Gisler. *Careers for Hard Hats & Other Construction Types*. 2nd ed. New York, NY: McGraw-Hill, 2010.

Facts on File. *Construction*. New York, NY: Infobase Publishing, 2010.

Farr, Michael. *Best Jobs for the 21st Century*. 4th ed. Indianapolis, IN: JIST Publishing, 2006.

Federal Motor Carrier Program, U.S. Department of Transportation. "Commercial Driver's License Program (CDL/CDLIS)." Retrieved September 30, 2012 (http:// www.fmcsa.dot.gov/registration-licensing/cdl/cdl.htm).

Green Careers in Building and Landscaping. Lawrenceville, NJ: Peterson's, 2010.

Job Corps, U.S Department of Labor. "Job Corps Home Page." Retrieved September 30, 2012 (http://recruiting .jobcorps.gov/en/home.aspx).

Moore, Ron (general manager/cost estimator, Western Building Restoration). Interview with the author, September 28, 2012.

New Home Guide. "Home Building 101: Stages of Construction." Retrieved September 30, 2012 (http://www .newhomeguide.com/new-home-services-guide/buying-a -home/the-building-process/homebuilding-101.html).

O*Net. "Details Report for: 51-2041.00 - Structural Metal Fabricators and Fitters." Retrieved September 30, 2012 (http://www.onetonline.org/link/details/51-2041.00).

Owen, Ruth. *Building Green Places.* New York, NY: Crabtree Publishing Company, 2010.

StateUniversity.com. "Construction & Skilled Trades." Retrieved September 30, 2012 (http://careers.stateuniversity.com /collection/132/Construction.html#ixzz27vPqS8tt).

U.S. Census Bureau, U.S. Department of Commerce. "Statistics of U.S. Businesses," Retrieved September 30, 2012 (http://www.census.gov/econ/susb/index.html).

U.S. Department of Labor. "Become an Apprentice." Retrieved September 30, 2012 (http://www.labor.ny.gov /apprenticeship/general/registration.shtm).

White House. "Remarks by the President at the Building and Construction Trades Department Conference," Retrieved September 30, 2012 (http://www.whitehouse.gov/the -press-office/2012/04/30/remarks-president-building -and-construction-trades-department-conference).

index

ABOUT THE AUTHOR

Heather Moore Niver is a New York State author, editor, and poet. She has participated in juried writing workshops at the New York State Writer's Institute and the Edna St. Vincent Millay Society, and every winter she leads a writing workshop at an Adirondack arts retreat. She has written more than twenty nonfiction children's books about sports cars, marketing, animals, and more.

PHOTO CREDITS

Cover pkchai/Shutterstock.com; cover (background), p. 1 Bertold Werkmann/Shutterstock.com; p. 4 photobank.ch/Shutterstock.com; pp. 8–9 Lev Kropotov/Shutterstock.com; p. 11 Ghislain & Marie David de Lossy/Cultura/Getty Images; p. 14 Comstock Images/Thinkstock; p. 17 altrendo images/Stockbyte/Thinkstock; p. 19 Jupiterimages/Photos.com/Thinkstock; p. 23 Dmitry KalinovskyShutterstock.com; p. 27 kurhan/Shutterstock.com; p. 31 Zigy Kaluzny/Stone/Getty Images; p. 33 Vadim Ratnikov/Shutterstock.com; pp. 34–35 Image Source/Getty Images; p. 38 John Burke/Photolibrary/Getty Images; p. 40 auremar/Shutterstock.com; p. 43 Biddiboo/Stone/Getty Images; p. 45 Tetra Images/Getty Images; p. 49 Inga Ivanova/Shutterstock.com; pp. 52–53 Levent Konuk/Shutterstock,com; pp. 54–55 Digital Vision/Photodisc/Thinkstock; pp. 56–57 © iStockphoto.com/Justin Horrocks; pp. 60–61 Construction Jobs, Inc.; pp. 62–63 © iStockphoto.com/Photo_Alto; pp. 66–67 Fotosearch/Getty Images.

Designer: Nicole Russo; Editor: Nicholas Croce;
Photo Researcher: Marty Levick